FASHION IN
COLOR

FASHION IN COLOR

A JOURNEY THROUGH EVERY HUE

Megan Hess

Hardie Grant

BOOKS

For Martina Granolic

who mainly wears black but fills my entire
world with every inspiring color.

CONTENTS

INTRODUCTION

One of my roles as a fashion illustrator is to live-sketch fashion shows as they happen – and when a garment first appears on the runway, it's the *color* that first catches my eye. Color makes the opening statement, gives an immediate sense of mood, and draws me in to examine the piece. The form, line and texture are equally important, but color makes the first impression.

When we choose colors in fashion, there are so many contexts to consider. We might be thinking in relation to the season and occasion, such as selecting a serene blue gown for a summer evening, or a cozy brown knit for an autumn escape. We consider cultural associations, knowing a playful bright pink could remind people of Barbie, a rich gold suggests opulence, or pure white connotes bridal elegance. And we're also thinking of the color tones of the wearer, for example, how wonderfully jade green can go with flaming red hair.

Black, of course, is an important shade in fashion. Coco Chanel loved black and believed it 'accentuated the essential.' Black can convey a great range of meanings: it can be conservative and chic, dangerously seductive, or intelligent and rebellious. From Audrey Hepburn's Givenchy dress in *Breakfast at Tiffany's* to Christóbal Balenciaga's sculptural haute couture, to Versace's signature use of black and gold, designers have created iconic moments in black. However, I have focused on black in many of my books, so in this one I have chosen instead to focus on a bright and beautiful collection of color.

The book also touches on color in decor and branding. After all, Hermès Orange, Tiffany Blue and Harrods Green are such an important part of their brands' unique identity. Certain dresses and their distinctive colors have made a lasting mark in fashion history. For example, it's hard to see a white halter neck dress and *not* think of Marilyn Monroe pushing down her fluttering skirt. This book is a journey through color, including some of the fashion world's most iconic dresses, their designers, their wearers, and the impact they had.

Color can be playful, elegant, moody or dramatic. Color can express joy or grief. With the colors we choose, we are saying something unique about ourselves to the world.

01

FASHION IN

BLUE

Valentino

Blue

Blue often symbolizes a tranquillity and depth inspired by the sea and sky. From Grace Kelly's ice blue gown in *To Catch a Thief* to the powder blue Prada dress Lupita Nyong'o wore to the Oscars in 2014, blue has been worn as the color of grace and sophistication.

There is a romance behind the color blue associated with wealth, exotic lands and rare materials. In ancient times, the Egyptian blue used by the Pharaohs was made by heating a powder of sand, ash and copper in a furnace of more than 800° Celsius (1,472° Fahrenheit). Egyptian blue made a revival with the Art Deco movement in the 1920s, when designers fell in love with the aesthetics of Tutankhamun and the blue that set off the gold of his treasures.

Medieval Europe was obsessed with ultramarine blue, which was made from lapis lazuli, an expensive gemstone, mined in what is now north-east Afghanistan. Painters went into debt for the beautiful color, which was associated with opulence and purity, and at times it was more expensive than gold.

Tiffany Blue continues that classical connection between the color blue and a sense of preciousness and exclusivity.

BLUE

15

FASHION IN COLOR

The color blue conjures up wide-open spaces: the clear sky, the calm, shifting sea. An ocean can be anything from stormy to sun-kissed, tranquil turquoise to flashing sapphire.

The French Riviera will always be associated with oceanic blues. After all, it's called the *Côte d'Azur* for a reason. Traditionally the playground of the Parisian elite, the Riviera is known as a center for fashion. It was here that Coco Chanel adopted the blue Breton stripe from Gallic sailors' uniforms into luxury holiday-wear and *la marinière* went on to become a symbol of sophistication and leisure. The Breton stripe was worn, famously, by Brigitte Bardot and James Dean. It remains a nautical staple in any coastal holiday suitcase, just as the French Riviera will always be known for its turquoise blue scenery.

'There are connoisseurs of blue just as there are connoisseurs of wine.'

SIDONIE-GABRIELLE COLETTE

TIFFANY & CO.

The distinctive Tiffany Blue, like the blue of a robin's egg, is a Pantone shade patented as '1837 Blue', and has become synonymous with luxury and romance. The shade was unveiled in 1845 for their Tiffany Blue Book, initially a mail-order catalog, but now a high-end annual publication, showcasing their most spectacular work. A Tiffany Blue Box is instantly recognizable, and the color has transcended its packaging to embody the brand itself. Beyond aesthetics, there's a fascinating psychological link: studies suggest that women's heart rates increase by twenty per cent when they see a Tiffany Blue Box, underscoring the profound emotional impact associated with the brand.

From the days of Chanel creating the Breton stripe for the Riviera elites' leisure wear, generations of couturiers have taken the deep blue sea as their muse. It has inspired some wonderful designs, such as Alexander McQueen's 2010 Plato's Atlantis ready-to-wear collection, and Elie Saab and Zuhair Murad's 2019 homage to ocean life.

For anyone who watched *The Devil Wears Prada*, Meryl Streep's blistering but deeply informative speech about cerulean blue is burned into our minds: 'that sweater is not just blue', she tells her assistant played by Anne Hathaway, 'it's actually cerulean.'

CHANEL

22

'Be careful when you are selecting a blue to see it both in daylight and electric light because it changes very much.'

_____

CHRISTIAN DIOR

FASHION IN COLOR

GRACE KELLY

Grace Kelly was synonymous with the glamour of the Riviera. In Hitchcock's *To Catch a Thief* she starred as a young heiress, holidaying in this picturesque coastal paradise. In her first scene, Grace Kelly is unmissable in an ice-blue floor-length gown and blue chiffon scarf, created by famed costume designer Edith Head. Head was nominated for an Academy Award for Best Costume Design for this film. She was known for working in close consultation with the female stars she designed for (unlike some of her male contemporaries), which made her popular with stars like Ginger Rogers, Bette Davis, Audrey Hepburn and Elizabeth Taylor.

FASHION IN COLOR

BLUE

29

Several memorable blue gowns have glided on red carpets – think Nicole Kidman in a structured strapless cobalt dress by Armani Privé or Claire Danes, Cinderella-like at the Met Gala, in a glowing sky-blue Zac Posen gown. Lupita Nyong'o made an indelible mark on the fashion world at the 2014 Oscars, in a stunning custom Prada gown. The dress was also vibrant sky-blue, which Nyong'o said reminded her of her hometown Nairobi, in Kenya. The plunging neckline and flowing pleated skirt were a nod to Old Hollywood glamour and the dress won widespread acclaim in the fashion world.

BLUE

WEDGWOOD

Blue and white porcelain has a heritage going back to the Tang Dynasty in China, and is connected to Islamic ceramics by the cobalt trade from Persia. The delicate blue and white porcelains from China became highly sought after with the European well-to-do but were costly to import. In the mid-1700s, English potter Josiah Wedgwood was determined to create his own blue ceramic and, after thousands of experiments, developed blue Jasperware. The soft, pale shade is still known today as 'Wedgwood blue' and holds profound significance for the Wedgwood brand. Wedgwood blue symbolizes sophistication and elegance, recalling luxurious high teas, pretty English flowers and Wedgwood's early neo-classical designs.

BLUE

02

FASHION IN

GREEN

Mint tule

Green

Green is the color of lush foliage and is said to be soothing to the eye and the spirit. Green can also sparkle in jewel tones such as emerald and jade. Like the Irish shamrock, green can be considered lucky and is often associated with money and wealth, because it resembles the color of US banknotes.

Green is sometimes known as the color of jealousy and poison. In 1775 Scheele's Green was invented: a green pigment made with arsenic. It was an intoxicating bold green color the world fell in love with – and then died for. In the mid 1800s, use of the dye was banned in many countries, but an association with danger remained.

In the early days of Hollywood glamour, green held a particular place. Elizabeth Taylor was a regal Cleopatra in green and gold and Vivien Leigh wore luxurious green velvet in *Gone with the Wind*. In more recent years Keira Knightley wore an emerald green silk flapper dress in *Atonement* that took the fashion world by storm. Anya Taylor-Joy harked back to a classic Hollywood aesthetic in her green Dior dress for the 2021 Golden Globes.

GREEN

GUCCI

The Gucci brand has always used green. From their early days they used green in their ubiquitous stripe, alongside red and white, in the style of a high-quality luggage strap. This stripe references the colors of the Italian flag and Gucci's equestrian beginnings. Gucci often creates texture through pattern, using repeated monogramming and motifs, frequently in green.

Gucci also uses green in the decor of their boutiques, with green carpets or soft furnishings. Gucci has seen some significant dresses on the screen and the red carpet. Elle Fanning wore Gucci in romantic green with fairytale floral trimmings for the *Maleficent* premier. The brand's collaborations with Jessica Chastain prove the truism that redheads look stunning in green. Chastain wore a Gucci emerald silk lame bustier to the 2022 *Vanity Fair* Oscar party and donned a green Gucci gown again for the 25H Gucci Watch campaign. The bold contrast of her hair against the rich green of the fabric makes the images for this campaign both striking and beautiful.

GUCCI

HARRODS

London's luxury department store, Harrods traditionally uses deep green as a backing for their gold logo, and the color is so recognized that it's known as Harrods Green. Their iconic awnings are the same green with gold, as are the legendary Harrods doormen's uniforms. Harrods luxury tea comes in delicate green tins, and you can even purchase a Harrods teddy bear dressed in their green doorman uniform, or with a green Harrods bow around its cute little fuzzy neck.

42

43

In 2018 Giambattista Valli created a voluminous green tulle gown for his Paris Fashion Week spring/summer show. Giambattista Valli is well known for his use of tulle which balances ballet-dancer purity with tantalizing transparency, evoking femininity and romance. This particular dress used 350 meters of tulle. An article in *Elle* magazine marveled over the fact that if you held that vertically it would be 20 meters taller than the Eiffel Tower. On the runway, it was a billowing chartreuse concoction, like the frothy, feminine embodiment of spring.

GIAMBATTISTA VALLI

44

GREEN

'I love to see green used in every shade and in every material, from tweed in the morning to satin in the evening. There is green for everyone and for every complexion.'

CHRISTIAN DIOR

GREEN

FASHION IN COLOR

GREEN

In 2021 Anya Taylor-Joy was nominated for two Golden Globes – *The Queen's Gambit* and *Emma*. Lockdown meant there was no in-person red carpet event, but Taylor-Joy didn't let that hold her back. She donned a custom Dior haute couture green gown, in a style that rang with classic Hollywood glamour. The slinky emerald green gown, with a plunging neckline was paired with a matching floor-sweeping coat and Tiffany & Co. diamond jewelry. The dress was custom designed by Dior's creative director Maria Grazia Chiuri and styled by Law Roach. Fashion commentators from *Vogue* to *Harper's Bazaar* were full of glowing praise. It was called the dress that cemented Anya Taylor-Joy as a star.

DIOR

Green is the color of life, new growth and springtime. The tranquil color reminds us of verdant fields, pretty gardens, luxurious tropical forests. No wonder so many green colors are named for plant life. Words for colors like mint, sage, lime and forest green all come straight from nature's palette. Many alfresco dining places, like the Dior cafe in Saint-Tropez, make use of natural green surroundings to create a restorative retreat where visitors can unwind and refresh themselves.

'Green is the prime color of the world, and that from which its loveliness arises.'

CALDERÓN DE LA BARCA,
SPANISH POET

ZUHAIR
MURAD

Zuhair Murad's spring/summer 2023 show was inspired by the Belle Époque chateaus of the French Riviera, harking to their architectural designs and color schemes. One pale green ensemble from that show made its way to the red carpet, worn by Kate Beckinsale at the premier of *La Passion de Dodin Bouffant* (*The Taste of Things*). The beaded tulle jumpsuit is high-necked, long-sleeved and extra-short at the thigh, with a voluminous taffeta overskirt and an oversized ribbon gracing the waist.

FASHION IN COLOR

ELIE SAAB

At fifteen, Elie Saab moved from his village to the city of Beirut in war-torn Lebanon. Before the move he made dresses for his sisters. In the city, he began to make a living by selling his designs to the women of Beirut. After Saab's eventful early career in fashion, Halle Berry landed the designer on the world stage in 2002. She wore an astonishing Elie Saab dress, as the first Black woman to win an Academy Award for Best Actress for her role in *Monster's Ball*. The dress had a deep red sheer bodice, detailed with leafy green embroidery. The green detailing emphasized her figure while offering strategic concealment. After seeing Halle Berry in his dress, everyone wanted more Elie Saab.

Saab often works in shades of green, using sequins, embroidery and intricate beading, to create texture and interest in his timelessly elegant evening wear. He's been worn by Taylor Swift, Gwyneth Paltrow, Sarah Jessica Parker and Catherine Zeta-Jones – all in shades of green.

03

FASHION IN YELLOW

Yellow

Yellow is the color of youth and sunshine, of daffodils and sunflowers. Yellow is cheerful. It's buttercups, bumblebees and brass band instruments. It also has a place in the evening, being the color of warm candle flames, sparkling champagne and opulent gold.

Van Gogh loved using chrome yellow, a new pigment in his time. He contrasted yellow with blues over and over again: in *The Yellow House*, *The Night Café* and the swirling sky of *The Starry Night*. Van Gogh inspired designers like Yves Saint Laurent, Rodarte and Viktor &Rolf who have all created pieces that pay tribute to his yellow sunflowers.

Yellow has been worn by women who stood out from the crowd. Josephine Baker shook up 1920s Paris, in her yellow banana skirt. Michelle Williams accepted an Oscar for *Brokeback Mountain*, wowing the world in a saffron yellow Vera Wang gown. Emma Stone won an Academy Award as Best Actress for *La La Land,* where she tap-dances with Ryan Gosling wearing a canary yellow dress with a swinging skirt.

In the film clip to 'Hold Up', as part of her visual album *Lemonade*, Beyoncé wears a floating Roberto Cavalli mustard yellow dress. It lifts around her Saint Laurent Candy sandals as she strides down the street, joyfully and gracefully smashing car windows. Every scene in the song is marked with yellow accents. The album release sparked a renaissance in yellow as people were inspired by her look.

YELLOW

64

YELLOW

65

VERSAILLES

The Hall of Mirrors at the Palace of Versailles is a grand, baroque gallery designed by architect Jules Hardouin-Mansart and completed in 1684. It was created for King Louis XIV, the Sun King. The vibrant golden hues of the hall echo the sun and so honor the king. The hall is lined with gilded bronze statues, and the ceilings are decorated with rich golden cornices and detailed gilt mouldings. Themes of yellow dominate the artworks.

In the afternoon, deep yellow light from the setting sun floods in, lighting up the warm golden timbers of the parquetry floors and reflected back by the 357 mirrors. By night, the mirrors double the yellow flame of each candle in the crystal chandeliers.

YELLOW

Bold yellow has been a strong choice for Pierpaolo Piccioli's Valentino couture. He has used bright sunflower, fresh lemon and neon yellow for his sculptural creations. Known for his use of monochrome and color blocking, Valentino's yellow pieces command attention.

VALENTINO

YELLOW

70

YELLOW

71

Some of the grandest Parisian interiors are made even more opulent with yellow and gold accents. Buildings like the Palais Garnier and the Louvre have gilt mouldings around the ceilings, lavish golden embellishments and decorative gilt surfaces. Gold in interior design can signify ostentation and wealth. It is reflective and brightens a room, but unlike silver or mirrors, the yellow tone of gold adds warmth to the atmosphere.

PRESS FOR

YELLOW

73

VERSACE

Versace has a profound association with the color gold. Versace decor uses luxurious golden hues as either a base or an accent in their rugs, cushions or printed on their silks. While their logo, the classic Medusa head, is officially black, it often appears as gold, or as white on a gold background. Most styles of their La Medusa handbag display the logo in shining gold on the flap. Versace gold has an opulent feel and the Medusa, an ancient symbol of fatal beauty, reflects Versace's rich sense of history. Lovers of the brand adorn their whole world with Versace – accessories, interiors, and of course their wardrobe.

FASHION IN COLOR

CAROLINA HERRERA

In the climactic scene of *How to Lose a Guy in 10 Days*, Kate Hudson wears a slinky buttercup satin gown that has had a cultural impact far beyond the film. As Kate Hudson turns around, she shows off the crisscross straps over the ultra-low back, the pale yellow seeming to make her skin glow. The dress clings to her hips as she strides away from the man who has lied to her. Hudson's character wears the famous yellow diamond necklace designed by Harry Winston, which sold for US$5 million after the film. Karen Patch, the film's costume designer, worked with designer and fashion icon Carolina Herrera to perfectly match the dress to the necklace.

Elie Saab is known for his work experimenting with textures. His beading, sequins and embroidery add detail to a base of delicate fabrics which cling to the body and skim the floor. His elegant, feminine dresses come in earthy citrine, buttery yellow, rich gold and of course, sparkling yellow sequins.

ELIE SAAB

04

FASHION IN

ORANGE

Orange

Tangerine

The color orange embodies energy, warmth, and a touch of excitement. Orange can be used in many different styles, depending on the hue. At the turn of the seasons, fashion often mirrors nature's autumnal rich, warm tints, reminiscent of changing foliage, firesides, and a festive Halloween aesthetic. Orange can be cozy, paired with soft creams and natural browns. Orange can also be jewel-like, in an opulent taffeta gown fit for a queen (like Beyoncé).

Orange is the color of sunsets and the magical golden hour when soft beams seem to make everything glow. Orange is associated with luxury and craftsmanship through its association with Hermès and their signature orange boxes. We've seen wonderful orange creations by designers like Valentino and Zuhair Murad.

The color can be garish, like in high-visibility workwear or the prison uniforms of *Orange is the New Black*. This means orange is a bold, defiant color in some contexts, and couturiers such as Alexander McQueen and Jean Paul Gaultier play with the vivid statement it makes.

But let's not forget that orange can be adorably pretty when it comes in pastels, like coral, peach or honeycomb–the perfect shades for a spring garden party styled by Christian Dior.

ORANGE

87

The history of orange in fashion can be traced back to ancient times, where natural dyes from plants and minerals produced a spectrum of oranges, from subtle tangerine to ochre rust. Orange is sacred in some Eastern cultures, connected with perfection, fire and purity, leading to the striking saffron dye found in certain holy robes.

Orange was an important color for Pre-Raphaelite painters, who took the luxuriously red-haired artist and model Elizabeth Siddal as their muse. Most famously Siddal was the model for John Everett Millais's *Ophelia*.

88

ORANGE

During Beyoncé's *On the Run II* tour in 2018, the pop queen stepped out in different looks for almost every stage of the tour. In Paris she wowed the world in a tangerine Valentino gown that had been worn by supermodel Adut Akech for Valentino's autumn/winter 2018 show. The dress was a crinkly taffeta with huge sweeping skirts and oversized puffed sleeves, cinched at the waist with a matching orange bow. The artist sat on the edge of the stage, with the bright fabric gathered around her, to sing her ballad, 'Resentment'. She was a warm spot of light in a huge, darkened stadium.

VALENTINO

FASHION IN COLOR

The time just after sunrise, or just before sunset, when the sun bathes the world in a warm, amber glow, is known as the 'golden hour'. It's a beautiful time to be somewhere with a view – and an ideal time for photography. The warm light is even and diffuse, and shadows are soft. The fleeting radiance makes the skin luminously beautiful, glimmers through thin fabrics and turns hair into a halo. The natural light of golden hour can make a pretty outdoor photoshoot breathtakingly beautiful.

'There is no blue without yellow and without orange.'

VINCENT VAN GOGH

ZUHAIR
MURAD

Lebanese designer Zuhair Murad often uses textured monochrome for his elegant evening wear. While he may only use a single color, like peach or bold orange, the use of texture adds layers of detail and shape to his work. For example, soft, voluminous feathers against sparkling sequins on clinging sheer silk, or crystallized crepe with embroidered patterns covered by graceful, floating capes.

In 1994 the Hermès box won the luxury packaging Oscar award. Since then, every Hermès product has come packaged in their signature orange box with a chocolate brown Bolduc ribbon. Hermès packaging has become so iconic that people collect the packaging and incorporate it into their home as part of their decor – as display storage, or a lampstand that reflects the warmth of the light, or even as a towering, boxy Christmas tree.

More than any other designer, the color orange is associated with Hermès whose iconic orange shade is bright, bold and clear. Thierry Hermès began by making quality harnesses in Paris in 1837 and while the product has changed, their values of finesse, excellence and creativity have not.

It was in occupied Paris, during World War II, that Hermès began their long association with the color orange. At the time, with supply lines down, the only packaging to be found were boxes nobody else had wanted – a stack of bright orange cardboard. Hermès took this lack and made it a strength, claiming the distinctive color as their own.

Now we find Hermès orange in many of their ranges, like their silk scarves, suede boots, or the leather of their extremely exclusive Kelly handbags. Through Hermès, the warm citrus color of orange is now intimately associated with quality, luxury and craftsmanship.

HERMÈS

'Orange is red brought closer to humanity...'

WASSILY KANDINSKY

JEAN PAUL GAULTIER

Jean Paul Gaultier, known for his iconoclastic, punky play with colors, shapes and genders, has had some highlight moments using orange. His cone bra, made famous by Madonna in her 1990 *Blond Ambition* tour, had an iteration in orange velvet as part of a ruched corset dress. For his final runway show, Gaultier created an astonishing sculptural dress in orange macaw feathers.

As the costume designer for the movie *The Fifth Element*, Gaultier used orange as a touchstone color throughout. Milla Jovovich wears bright orange braces and has matching orange hair.

In 2023 Haider Ackermann designed a runway show for Gaultier and the result was a collection of sharp tailoring and elegant, geometric and asymmetric shapes. One stand-out piece is an orange body-hugging pantsuit with an oversized bow at the waist. It's stunning, and speaks to Gaultier's use of orange over decades.

05

FASHION IN PINK

Vintage Dior

Pink

Depending on its shade, pink can express soft femininity or be a bold statement. Christian Dior's affinity for pink is well known, tracing back to the pink walls of his childhood home. The color is inextricably tied to Barbie, symbolizing glamour and girlish dreams. Pink reigns as the color of romance, and prettiness. Memorable moments for pink on the runway include Chanel's pink bride and Valentino's Pink PP collection.

The English word 'pink' comes from a type of flower called pinks (from the species *Dianthus*) but the word didn't used to mean the *color*. It first referred to the frilly edges of the pink flower's petals. We still use this meaning with the 'pinking shears', used in dressmaking to cut a zigzag line.

Pink has had some key moments in film. Marilyn Monroe's pink silk dress in *Gentlemen Prefer Blondes* was designed by William Travilla at the very last minute, for her performance of 'Diamonds are a girl's best friend'. The scene has been copied and re-imagined numerous times, memorably by Madonna for her 'Material girl' film clip.

In 2001, *Legally Blonde* introduced the world to Elle Woods, the charming, feminine and devastatingly clever Harvard law student, whose signature pink was a touchstone for the movie design. The costumes, by designer Sophie de Rakoff Carbonell, have influenced fashion since the film was released.

VINTAGE BARBIE

Barbie has always been associated with the color pink. On her release in 1959, Barbie's logo was a soft pink cursive on a white background. The logo was designed by Ruth Handler, the maker of Barbie. Handler was deeply interested in haute couture, and Barbie's fashion choices were as wonderful as her career choices. When all other dolls were babies, designed for little girls to practice mothering, Barbie was stepping out into the world as an astronaut, a flight attendant or a presidential nominee, and always devastatingly stylish.

Ever since her first release, the Barbie logo and packaging have never shifted away from the color pink. Barbie's dream house, campervan and car were all a vibrant, exciting pink. The Barbie-verse, in all its screen iterations, is flooded with pink. When images of Margot Robbie as Barbie in a hot pink western outfit were released in the lead-up to the release of Greta Gerwig's 2023 *Barbie* movie, online searches for pink clothes skyrocketed.

Costume designer Jacqueline Durran worked with Chanel to create some of the pieces for the movie, which was a candy-land fantasy dream in pink. With the movie's release, the use of pink ricocheted through fashion choices worldwide.

DIOR

Christian Dior's childhood home was a Belle Époque villa looking out over the ocean and inspired his designs for decades. The pale pink and gray of the walls made their way into his work and are still signature colors for the Dior brand today.

The English garden around the villa, planted by his mother Madeleine, was full of pink roses and lilies of the valley. These were an ongoing inspiration to Dior, who created his New Look collection with some of these flowers in mind. Christian Dior loved to use pinks in a way that was romantic, lavish and feminine.

'Every woman should have something pink in her wardrobe. It is the color of happiness and of femininity.'

CHRISTIAN DIOR

PINK

113

FASHION IN COLOR

Giambattista Valli's spring/summer 2023 season unfolded as a pastel dream, much of it in shades of sugary pink, that celebrated prettiness and soft feminine beauty. Valli's color palette for this season was inspired by the atmosphere of Beverly Hills, and in particular the Beverly Hills Hotel, which is known for its design in pink and green, and for its star-studded guest list. The collection showcased his signature mastery of using tulle and taffeta to sculpt garments with voluminous grace.

GIAMBATTISTA VALLI

118

Pink is the color of romance. It has been associated with pretty florals since ancient times, as flowers are one of the few places the color occurs in nature. Cherry blossoms, roses, peonies, begonias and carnations all give us pretty shades of pink. Pink also recalls the hues of sunset and sunrise – those moments when the sun's light is soft, turning clouds into candy floss, and water into rose gold. Pink can also be romantically sensuous, reminding us of soft lips and blushed cheeks.

'The color flashed in front of my eyes. Bright, impossible, impudent ...'

ELSA SCHIAPARELLI

'Anything is possible with sunshine and a little pink.'

LILLY PULITZER

PINK

122

VALENTINO

Valentino Couture's autumn/winter 2022/23 season was a visual ode to the power of pink monochrome. Creative director Pierpaolo Piccioli unveiled the Valentino Pink PP collection during Paris Fashion Week, showcasing a Pantone custom shade of hot, bold pink. With the show's palette so intensely limited, the shape and texture of each garment came into focus. Each look was different, from floaty and gauzy to tailored and sharp, from feathered and sequinned to soft, slouchy knits – but each look was entirely pink. The impact was dramatic and since the runway show, Ariana Grande, Florence Pugh, Anne Hathaway and other luminaries have donned Valentino's Pink PP ensembles. The collection's impact and continuing star power solidified pink's place as a force to be reckoned with in high couture.

Traditionally, the last look of a runway show is a bridal dress. This is not the case for all runways but generally for Haute Couture shows. The model wears the most sumptuous outfit of the season, which is, customarily, white. But sometimes designers play with the color scheme – and the Chanel bride has worn pink more than once (Devon Akoi and Edie Campbell were both pink Chanel brides). In 2017 Lily-Rose Depp made headlines as a gorgeous bride in pale pink, escorted down the runway by designer Karl Lagerfeld. The dress had dramatically ruffled skirts and sleeves, a buttoned, corseted bodice cinched at the waist with a belt, and a sweet Peter Pan collar. This unconventional but utterly beautiful pièce de résistance of the season left an indelible impression on the fashion world.

CHANEL

06

FASHION IN

RED

Cartier

Cruella

Vintage Dior

Red

The color red holds a particular status in the world of fashion. Cartier's signature red serves as a symbol of opulence and excellence. The red sequinned gown Marilyn Monroe wears in *Gentlemen Prefer Blondes* signifies passion and desire, while Audrey Hepburn's red dress in *Funny Face* captures a joyful elegance. Christian Louboutin's red-soled shoes and Valentino's vibrant red gowns have become synonymous with luxury and sophistication. Across the eras, red in fashion has signified power, romance, danger, passion and a bold expression of individuality.

The fashion house Valentino has used red as its signature color since its first show in the spring/ summer of 1959. From the 'Fiesta' red tulle cocktail dress in its very first show, to its extravagantly red Chinese New Year collection in 2024, Valentino has created in shades of red. Since their beginnings, the fashion house has used more than 550 hues of red in their designs. Penélope Cruz, Anne Hathaway, Joy Bryant, Scarlett Johansson and Iman have all worn Rosso Valentino on the red carpet.

Valentino Garavani said, 'For the Valentino Maison, red is not just a color. It is a non-fading mark, a logo, an iconic element of the brand, a value.'

132

The Cartier red box, with its golden garland inlay and cut corners, dates back to the early years of the Cartier Maison in Paris. The box itself is a collectable item and Cartier has made the deep red part of their branding, from the awnings of their New York flagship store, to the red carpet of their Paris boutique, to the red-and-gold military uniform worn by their staff.

In the 1966 movie *How to Steal a Million*, Eli Wallach, as a society art collector, proposes to Audrey Hepburn's character by tossing her a red Cartier box. The huge sparkling diamond nestled within sends her dizzily into the next farcical scene in the comedy caper. The movie credits Cartier in the opening: 'Miss Hepburn's jewelry by CARTIER, PARIS'.

In 2018, Cartier debuted their Guirlande de Cartier handbag at Paris Fashion Week, inspired by their signature jewelry box. The gem of a bag was splashed across fashion socials everywhere and was declared the 'it-bag' of the season.

CARTIER

137

AUDREY HEPBURN

In *Funny Face*, Audrey Hepburn's character Jo is a drab bookseller with a 'funny face' and no interest in fashion. She's convinced by a fashion photographer, Dick (played by Fred Astaire) to come to Paris and model for him. Dick bossily directs Jo in a sequence of photoshoots through famous Parisian locations. This culminates with Jo taking control of the shoot, in a scene at the Louvre. Here, she chooses her own moment and floats down the stairs in a stunning, floor length, red silk Givenchy gown. She holds up a sheer red scarf which flutters behind her. Dick tells her to stop, and her brilliant smile lights up the screen as she calls, 'I don't want to stop. I like it! Take the picture, take the picture!'

'Bright reds – scarlet, pillar-box red, crimson or cherry – are very cheerful and youthful. There is certainly a red for everyone.'

CHRISTIAN DIOR

In the opening scene of *Gentlemen Prefer Blondes*, Marilyn Monroe appears on stage as a showgirl, with her co-star Jane Russell, in scintillating red sequins to perform their charming, gold-digger origin story - 'Two little girls from Little Rock'.

The red dresses were designed by William Travilla, who designed costumes for Marilyn Monroe in eight movies. Each dress included a scattering of beige sequins, which look odd in real life, but on screen add to the wonderful sparkle of the gowns. Marilyn's gown from this scene was sold at auction for $250,000 in 2019.

MARILYN MONROE

145

'A thimbleful of red is redder than a bucketful.'

HENRI MATISSE

In *Pretty Woman*, Julia Roberts's character Vivian's transformative moment happens as she appears in a red dress. From her life as an L.A. call girl, Vivian's fairytale turns her into an elegant woman who dons a red evening gown and sparkling ruby necklace, before being flown to the opera. The off-the-shoulder dress, designed by Marilyn Vance, had a sweetheart neckline, a low back and ruffled detailing around the sleeves. In it, Julia Roberts steals the show and, after the movie's release, *Vogue* and *Harper's Bazaar* sang the dress's praises. More than three decades on, the dress still makes lists of most iconic dresses of all time.

PRETTY WOMAN

CRUELLA

Emma Stone stars as Cruella in the eponymous movie, telling the origin story of the villain from *101 Dalmatians*. Cruella lives amongst the 70s punk scene in London and works in a fashion house. In one extraordinary moment, she attends a black-and-white themed ball in a white satin cape, which she dramatically burns to nothing with the drop of a match. Beneath the cape is revealed an asymmetric blood-red dress twisted closely around her body and draping to the floor. Costume designer Jenny Beavan worked on the dress with cutter Ian Wallace, inspired by the spiral designs of British–American fashion designer Charles James. The dress resonated for fashion lovers around the world and costume versions of it are available from all corners of the internet.

07

FASHION IN

PURPLE

Valentino

Purple

Purple can be feminine and floral in pale hues like lavender and lilac. It can be bold and bright, like in fuchsia and violet or dark and sombre in shades of grape and plum.

In the era of Cleopatra and Julius Caesar, purple dye was created using a kind of shellfish, in a demanding process that meant the dye was extremely precious. At times it was worth its weight in gold. Thus, purple became associated with power and royalty, and can signify wealth and extravagance. It also has links with magic and feminine power.

Purple has had some celebrated moments on film and on the runway: from Eva Green in a plunging purple silk dress in *Casino Royale*, to Sandra Bullock in *Miss Congeniality* wearing a ruched purple mini dress as she slow-motion struts towards the camera. In 2022 Pantone's release of 'Very Peri', sitting somewhere between periwinkle and hot violet, made waves on the runway – with houses such as Gucci, Valentino and Saint Laurent all showing monochrome ensembles in the bold color.

156

VALENTINO

The Italian designer Valentino has created many stunning masterpieces using bold, rich purples. Florence Pugh, Lady Gaga and Naomi Campbell have all chosen purple Valentino dresses to wear on the red carpet.

PURPLE

159

160

Christian Dior thought we should be careful about wearing purple, saying that it worked best on complexions that were either very dark or very fair. But the designer loved soft pastel hues and used purple in these pretty, feminine shades. He was inspired by the sweet flowers his mother loved – and purple floral references weave their way gently through his designs. Even decades after his tragic death, the brand harks back to Dior's love of floral purple – with notable offerings like their lavender Lady Dior bag and their sparkling Purple Oud scent.

DIOR

FASHION IN COLOR

Purple adds an element of decadence to high teas, with treats like sugared violets, lilac macarons, mulberry meringues and cupcakes with creamy purple frosting layered prettily on tiered platters.

These kinds of confectionaries inspired the costume designer for Sofia Coppola's 2006 film *Marie Antoinette*. Apparently, Coppola gifted the costume designer Milena Canonero a box of macarons, saying that these were the colors she loved. Canonero then based the palette for the costume design on the sweet, pastel-colored treats. Milena Canonero won an Oscar for *Marie Antoinette*, which is a work of high fashion, as pretty and extravagant as a platter of purple macarons.

In real life, Queen Marie Antoinette introduced a new color to the court – a kind of purplish brown. When he first saw it, her husband said it was 'couleur de puce!', which means the 'color of fleas'. This isn't necessarily as unpleasant as it sounds, as 'ma petit puce' (my little flea) is a French term of endearment, like the English might use 'lovebug'. The name for the color stuck, and puce shot into fashion – by all reports, it was the color everyone wore in 1775.

Pastel purples are a classic color for interiors of stately homes. Ladies' boudoirs and morning rooms might be done out in pretty lilac and lavender. English manor interiors often featured muted pastel color palettes like chalky purples, inspired by the landscape. They used soft purples in their wallpaper, silk cushions and damask drapery. Pale purple decor can bring an elegant but gentle feeling of springtime and florals into the home.

PURPLE

'I was a punk before it got its name. I had that hairstyle and purple lipstick.'

VIVIENNE WESTWOOD

Giambattista Valli often crafts dresses in a single color, and his style works beautifully in purples like lilac or violet. Using skilful techniques with tulle ruffles, or generous silk drapery, he adds depth and sculptures shapes in his work. His monochromatic approach directs attention to the meticulously crafted design, showcasing Valli's mastery of form and texture.

GIAMBATTISTA VALLI

08

FASHION IN

BROWN

Brown

The color brown is versatile and timeless. It can have a natural sense of the rugged outdoors, recalling rich earth and strong tree trunks. It can be nutty and autumnal, warm, grounded and solid. But brown also encompasses luxury, from the rich spicy brown of cinnamon to dark chocolate and pale caramel. Like a fine whisky or a golden honey, brown embodies sophistication.

In the 1920s, Art Deco glamour had a love affair with brown, using beige, taupe and bronze with gold tones in monochrome geometric designs. Brown took centrestage again in 1970s fashion when it was paired with strong oranges and greens, and decor was marked by ochre and terracotta. In 2021 fashion publications from *Vogue* to *Harper's Bazaar* to *Elle* were declaring brown the color of the season. But some of our most beloved luxury designers have had brown built into their brand since their earliest days: think Burberry, Louis Vuitton, Bally and Gucci.

Even outside its heydays, the fashion world has accessorized with brown. Perhaps with a classic camel trench, a chestnut leather tote or a pair of snappy brown suede ankle boots. This is because brown pairs so beautifully with other colors, making it a versatile neutral. Brown accessories can be investment pieces. Brown also has a timeless place in leisurely summer elegance, where pale sand browns pair with cream linens, rattan bags and espadrilles.

178

GUCCI

Brown has been an important color for Gucci since the brand's beginnings making leather luggage and saddles. Gucci's classic monogram-patterned canvas is two interlocking Gs in brown on beige, often paired with brown leather detailing. Gucci have a history of using their branding and shades of brown to create pattern and texture.

Gucci worked as a hotel porter at London's Savoy, acquiring a knowledge of British high society (and their luggage) before he opened his own workshop, taking Italy's heritage leather industry into the world of high fashion. Gucci's timeless designs still speak to that heritage, and today's Gucci brown duffel would not have seemed out of place if it had arrived in a suite of the London Savoy in the early 1900s.

FASHION IN COLOR

The identity of French luxury fashion house, Louis Vuitton was built around a monogram pattern in shades of brown on their luxury luggage. The monogram of an interlocking L and V, combined with quatrefoils and flowers was initially created to defeat imitations. Since its launch, the iconic brown patterning has been an essential part of the Louis Vuitton brand. Louis Vuitton has designed products in varying shades and patterns of brown that accentuate and differentiate their logo. In doing so, they have retained the same essence in their timeless aesthetic for over a century.

Today we see the classic Louis Vuitton branding, with their monogram patterning in shades of brown, on all kinds of lifestyle products, from sunglasses cases and tennis racquet covers to skateboards, teddy bears and dumbbells. This is a brand that is built around its ethos of the spirit of travel.

LOUIS VUITTON

BALLY

Bally, the luxury Swiss brand, began by crafting shoes –
so shades of brown leather have always been core to its
identity. It is a joy to wear their timeless footwear and
bags, which often come in quiet browns and are elegant
but also neutral, meaning you can pair them with anything
from gentle cream to shocking pink. Bally also reveals how
lovely a warm, pale brown can be in decor; brown features
in the timber fittings of Bally's flagship stores, generating
a deep sense of calm as soon as you step inside. Bally are
known for their collaborations with artists, from the bold
poster designer Bernard Villemot in the sixties to the
defiant street aesthetics of graffiti artist Andre Saraiva and
aerosol x-ray artist Shok-1. Most of all, Bally are known for
their craftmanship, which is always in fashion.

BROWN

187

Because of its natural coloring, brown has a peaceful, natural feel and is an easy choice when designing alfresco entertaining. Elegant open-air dining spaces often use brown timber as a neutral against luxurious greens and florals, such as The Ivy Chelsea Garden, London or the Pavillion de la Fontaine in the Jardin du Luxembourg, Paris. Natural resources like wood and sand have a special place in decor. Sandstone bathrooms and warm timber floorboards bring a touch of opulence to a home. Walnut paneling and mahogany furniture invest an interior with a sense of heritage luxury.

189

GIAMBATTISTA VALLI

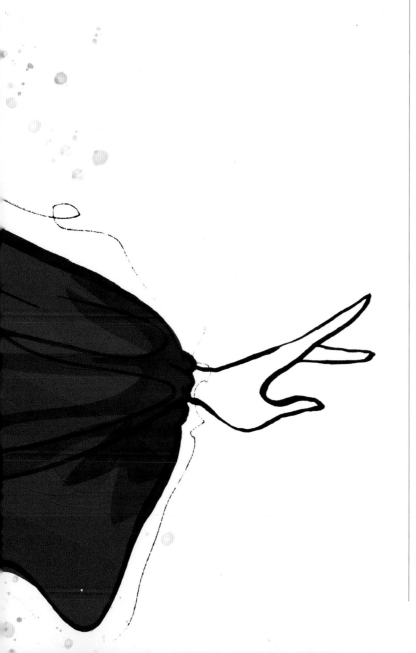

Zendaya, a style icon with an incredible acting career, has made a habit of bringing brown dresses to the red carpet. She stepped out in a tan Balmain dress with a thigh-high slit to the premier of *Dune*, and a chocolate Valentino bubble hem dress at the Venice Film Festival. A light brown leather and lace vintage Versace couture gown hugged her figure at the Las Vegas CinemaCon's Big Screen Achievement Awards. Perhaps the most outstanding example of Zendaya in brown is the sumptuous, off-the-shoulder chocolate chiffon gown by Giambattista Valli that she wore as a presenter for the 2018 Oscars, paired with exquisite Bulgari diamond earrings.

'Through the application of brown, an indescribably inner beauty is created.'

WASSILY KANDINSKY

BURBERRY

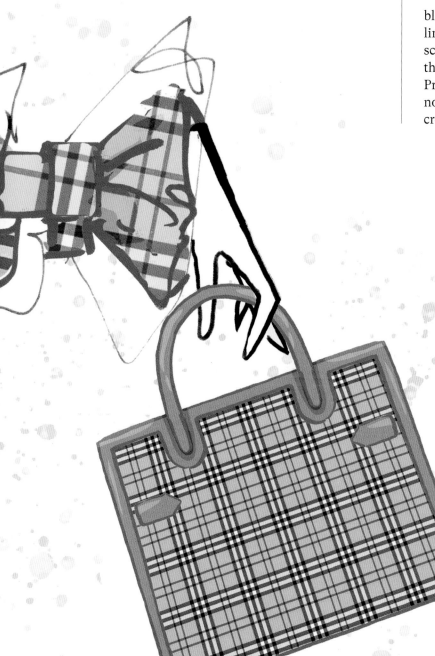

Brown is a signature color of Burberry, who have been dressing members of high society in quality camel and khaki for more than a century. In their early days, the brand outfitted polar explorers and provided trench coats for the British Army. In 1955 they were granted a Royal Warrant as weather proofer to the Royal Family.

The Burberry plaid, a soft, pale brown intersected with black, white and red, was originally used as a trench coat liner, but was so beloved that it burst out on umbrellas, scarves and exterior wear. Burberry was the darling of the 'Sloane set' in the late 70s, typified by the ever-stylish Princess Diana in a camel Burberry trench. Burberry is now a global luxury fashion creator, and their iconic creamy brown is a core part of the Burberry brand.

Brown is used with sophistication and subtle elegance in cosmetics. From eyeshadow, to bronzer, to lipstick, there are shades of brown to go beautifully with every skin tone. Blushers might be burned browns with undertones of red or pink, chocolaty brown mascaras can be used for a natural daytime look and a smouldering smoky-eye might use cool dark browns. Who can go past a Dior eye palette of minerally browns or the soft brown bristles of a Hermès make-up brush?

196

09

FASHION IN

WHITE

Valentino

White

WHITE

White signifies purity, innocence and peace. White can be angelic, ethereal and has links with the divine. It is, of course, bridal, recalling elaborate gowns, and the magic of 'happily ever after'. In haute couture, white might recall elements of the natural world, like apple blossoms and lilies, snow, seafoam, polar bears or peace doves.

White is often considered sophisticated. Historically, wearing white was associated with wealth, as it showed the wearer didn't work in dirty places. Today, white has its practical uses; white deflects the summer heat, and it also acts as a reflector, subtly lighting up the face. It can be a canvas that makes any other color stand out. It can be a neutral and has its place in daily wear – think crisp white button-up shirts, wide-leg linen pants or clean white sneakers. White dresses have had some spectacular moments on screen – worn by icons like Marilyn Monroe and Grace Kelly.

WHITE

White is a classic choice for spring and summer wardrobes.
White goes with pretty florals and garden summer
greenery. In the scorching heat, white reflects sunlight,
keeping us simultaneously cool and stylish. Linen, in
cream, white and ivory, allows skin to breathe in the
summer breeze and its natural texture adds depth to white
ensembles. A white dress captures the essence of carefree
spring days and can contrast with a warm summer tan.
On a warm day, white is both simple and sophisticated.

Dior

PRADA

VALENTINO

CHANEL

CHANEL

208

WHITE

If Marilyn Monroe is known by any single image alone, it's the moment in a white halter-neck cocktail dress, where a breeze lifts her pleated skirt in a billowing fan. The scene is from the movie, *The Seven Year Itch*, set in an oppressively hot summer in New York, where Marilyn's character is delighted to stand over a subway grate and feel the cooling updraft from a passing train. She appears innocently relieved by the breeze, while her companion (along with the camera) enjoys a tantalizing view of her gorgeous legs. Designer William Travilla said he wanted Monroe to look 'cool and clean in a dirty, dirty city.' The scene was initially shot on location in New York just after midnight, but a crowd of fans gathered to watch. Their noisy enthusiasm made filming tricky. Despite trying for fourteen takes, the scene needed to be reshot in the quiet of a 20th Century Fox studio. The dress has had a legacy of countless tributes and references – from oversized statues to red carpet imitations. There is even a collector's edition Marilyn Barbie. The dress sold for US$2.5 million at auction in 2011.

MARILYN MONROE

212

'White is pure and simple and matches with everything.'

CHRISTIAN DIOR

214

GRACE KELLY

In *To Catch a Thief*, Grace Kelly wears white in the fireworks scene. Costume designer Edith Head dressed her in a strapless, Grecian-style, floor-length gown with a diaphanous, floating skirt. In this scene, Grace Kelly plays the temptress – trying to convince Cary Grant's character to admit that he is a diamond thief. The romantic tension sparks, like the fireworks in the sky beyond them, and the diamond necklace glitters against her bare skin offset by her elegant white dress.

FASHION IN COLOR

Although Coco Chanel is best known for her love of black, white was also important to her. Chanel herself often wore the color, and her spring show in 1933 was a collection all in white. White was used as an accent in her looks - like white pearls on a little black dress, a white petal collar on a black gown, or white trimming on a black suit. Since then, cream and white have been pivotal elements in Chanel's brand identity. Chanel uses a strategic interplay of black and white in their store decor and packaging. White or cream frequently play a crucial role in the iconic Chanel tweed, adding texture or accents to pink or black or orange. White is a key element of Chanel's crisp designs, creating interesting textures and emphasizing clean lines.

'I have said that black has it all. White too. Their beauty is absolute. It is the perfect harmony.'

COCO CHANEL

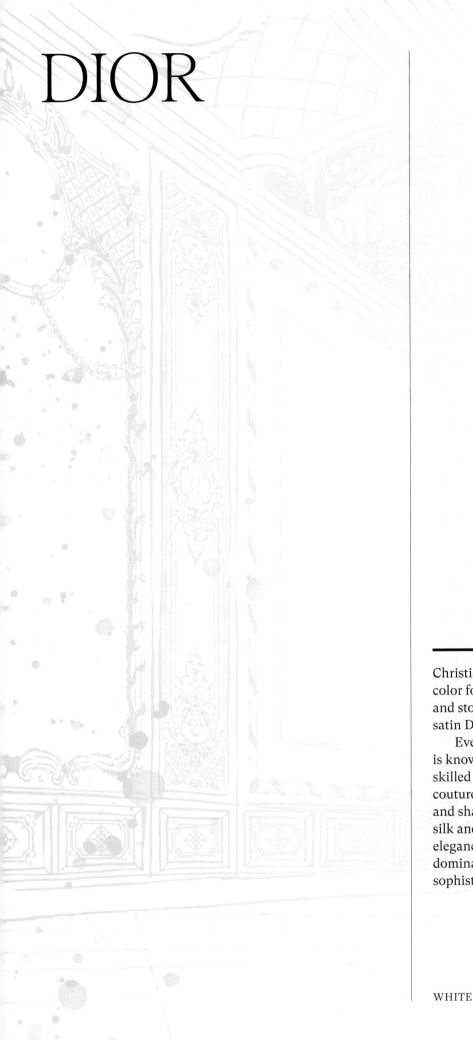

DIOR

Christian Dior thought that white was the most beautiful color for evening wear. He said it was pure and simple and stood out in a crowd. Grace Kelly danced in a white satin Dior gown at her engagement ball.

Even working in monochrome white, the Dior brand is known for creating contrasting textures and using skilled techniques to create drama in their designs. In Dior couture, layers and lace, pleats and paneling add texture and shape to a female silhouette. Dior's creations in white silk and tulle over decades celebrate a pure feminine elegance and grace. Dior's 2023 Fall couture range was dominated by white monochrome, celebrating the simple sophistication of Greek and Roman antiquity.

MICHELLE OBAMA

In 2009 Michelle Obama made her first appearance as America's First Lady at the Inaugural Ball, wearing an ivory off-the-shoulder silk gown detailed with organza rosettes, Swarovski crystals and thread of silver embroidery. It was designed by Jason Wu, who was only twenty-six years old at the time and relatively unknown. She looked stunning. The white of the gown symbolized hope and newness. Wu shot to fame as images of the gown hit the press. The dress is now displayed at the Smithsonian's National Museum of America alongside other First Ladies' inaugural gowns going back to 1912.

WHITE

221

ACKNOWLEDGMENTS

To Antonietta Anello, for editing and overseeing this book from its initial concept to its glorious finish.

To Martina Granolic, thank you for diving into the color wheel of fashion and poring over every detail to make this book so special.

To Ailsa Wild, thank you for investigating every single color with more detail than the F.B.I! You found so many beautiful and emotional elements of every color, thank you.

To Staci Barr, thank you for all your incredible help on the color mood boards - you always make everything better.

To Missy Lewis, thank you for all your beautiful work on our endpapers. Every gorgeous handbag in every gorgeous color!

To Murray Batten, another book together and once again you've brought every single color to life with your wonderful design and eye for detail.

To Todd Rechner, for your incredible care and attention in seeing my books to their finished form. You've made each book something precious to hold, to read, to keep forever. Thank you.

To my husband Craig and my children Gwyn and Will, thank you for making my life a rainbow of happiness.

ABOUT
THE AUTHOR

Megan Hess was destined to draw. An initial career in graphic design evolved into art direction for some of the world's leading advertising agencies and for Liberty London. In 2008, Megan illustrated Candace Bushnell's number-one-bestselling book *Sex and the City*. This catapulted Megan onto the world stage, and she began illustrating portraits for *The New York Times*, *Vogue Italia*, *Vanity Fair* and *TIME*, who described Megan's work as 'love at first sight'.

Today, Megan is one of the world's most sought-after fashion illustrators, with a client list that includes Givenchy, Tiffany & Co., Valentino, Louis Vuitton and *Harper's Bazaar*. Megan's iconic style has been used in global campaigns for Fendi, Prada, Cartier, Dior and Salvatore Ferragamo. She has illustrated live for fashion shows such as Fendi at Milan Fashion Week, Chopard at the 2019 Cannes Film Festival, Viktor & Rolf and Christian Dior Couture.

Megan has created a signature look for Bergdorf Goodman, New York, and a bespoke bag collection for Harrods of London. She is also the Global Artist in Residence for the prestigious Oetker Hotel Collection.

Megan illustrates all her work with a custom Montblanc pen that she affectionately calls 'Monty'.

Megan has written and illustrated over twelve bestselling fashion books, as well as her much-loved series for children, *Claris: the Chicest Mouse in Paris*.

When she's not in her studio working, you'll find Megan dreaming about every color in the rainbow and which color pen she'll pick up next!

Visit Megan at meganhess.com

Published in 2024 by Hardie Grant Books, an imprint of Hardie Grant Publishing

Hardie Grant Books (Melbourne)
Wurundjeri Country
Building 1, 658 Church Street
Richmond, Victoria 3121

Hardie Grant North America
2912 Telegraph Ave
Berkeley, California 94705

hardiegrant.com/books

Hardie Grant acknowledges the Traditional Owners of the Country on which we work,
the Wurundjeri People of the Kulin Nation and the Gadigal People of the Eora Nation,
and recognises their continuing connection to the land, waters and culture.
We pay our respects to their Elders past and present.

 A catalogue record for this
book is available from the
NATIONAL
LIBRARY   National Library of Australia
OF AUSTRALIA

Fashion in Color: A journey through every hue
ISBN 978 1 74379 736 5

10 9 8 7 6 5 4 3 2 1

Publisher: Roxy Ryan
Head of Editorial: Jasmin Chua
Project Editor: Antonietta Anello
Researcher: Ailsa Wild
Designer: Murray Batten
Design Manager: Kristin Thomas
Head of Production: Todd Rechner
Production Controller: Jessica Harvie

Color reproduction by Splitting Image Colour Studio
Printed in China by Leo Paper Products LTD.

The paper this book is printed on is from FSC®-certified forests and other
sources. FSC® promotes environmentally responsible, socially beneficial
and economically viable management of the world's forests.